**Other titles in the UWAP Poetry series
(established 2016)**

Our Lady of the Fence Post by J. H. Crone

Border Security by Bruce Dawe

Melbourne Journal by Alan Loney

Star Struck by David McCooey

Dark Convicts by Judy Johnson

Rallying by Quinn Eades

Flute of Milk by Susan Fealy

A Personal History of Vision by Luke Fischer

Snake Like Charms by Amanda Joy

Charlie Twirl by Alan Gould

Afloat in Light by David Adès

Communists Like Us by John Falzon

Hush by Dominique Hecq

Praise for previous publications:

'With its beer-drenched Blundstones, cricket balls retrieved from neighbour's backyards, misbehaving pastor's kids and crabs plucked from the Moyne River, O'Reilly's poetry collects and curates a series of vernacular objects and experiences that comprise life in Australia and beyond. From the streets of Ballarat to the dry highways of West Texas, from the floor of a petrol station in rural NSW to the evening sky seen from a Scottish beach, this poetry traverses continents, testing spaces and locations and finding them brimming with their own types of desire. Using a light touch and an elegant voice, *Distance* traces out nostalgia's peculiar contours and emotional resonances, resulting in remarkable poetic moments that will return and whisper again to a reader even after the book is set down.'—LACHLAN BROWN, author of *Limited Cities*

'*Distance* is a hugely nostalgic collection, traditionally, elegantly and simply (in the best sense of the word) written. Marked by a sense of both internal and external exploration, the poems take us on a journey through time and place, charting the terrain of identity, nationality, connection and belonging within the context of spatial, cultural and temporal displacement. These poems have the power to make one pine for one's own childhood, reassess one's own identity, and reconsider one's own connection to "ancestors" and "country."'—MICHELE SEMINARA, author of *Engraft* and editor of *Verity La*

'Joseph Brodsky, the Russian Nobel laureate, once remarked that memory and art have in common the "ability to select, a taste for detail." In the work of Nathanael O'Reilly, memory and art come together to bring us poems that remember what cannot – what must not – be forgotten, in rich and telling detail and with a taste for quiet but incisive irony.'—PAUL KANE, author of *Welcome Light, Work Life* and *Australian Poetry: Romanticism and Negativity*

'Nathanael O'Reilly's poems sound the major themes of Australian poetry: landscape, displacement, yearning, and above all a critique of cultural narrowness. O'Reilly's plain spoken diction is often laced with understated wit, but is given ballast by its principled grounding in lived experience.'—NICHOLAS BIRNS, editor of *Antipodes*

'These wonderfully crafted narrative poems capture the diasporic identity, somewhere between home and elsewhere, a metaphor for the unknown. I particularly enjoy their realism, the way in which they evoke the yearning for a reckless, peripatetic youth spent in rural towns, for teenage friendships, mateships, encounters with, or dreams of post-pubescent love. I like the arrangement of the poems too; it's a fine, understated debut.'—MICHELLE CAHILL, author of *The Accidental Cage, Ophelia in Harlem* and *Vishvarupa*

'With an unmistakable Australian sensibility, O'Reilly summons the courage to face the places he's left behind in these frank, but as often heartfelt poems. Readers both near to, and far away from, the particulars here will easily and equally relate as he mines the things, boyhood, sport, car trips, girls, that are familiar to growing up everywhere and with language that feels completely true.'—JONATHAN BENNETT, author of *Here is My Street, This Tree I Planted* and *Civil and Civic*

'Poetry rich with imagery but controlled by emotional truth...a potent poetic combination.'—E. A. GLEESON, author of *In Between the Dancing* and *Maisie and the Black Cat Band*

Nathanael O'Reilly

Nathanael O'Reilly was born in Warrnambool in 1973 and raised in Ballarat, Brisbane and Shepparton. He attended university at Monash and Ballarat before moving overseas in 1995; he has travelled on five continents and spent extended periods in England, Ireland, Germany, Ukraine and the United States, where he currently resides. O'Reilly is the author of the full-length collection *Distance* and the chapbooks *Cult, Suburban Exile* and *Symptoms of Homesickness*. He is a recipient of an Emerging Writers' Grant from the Literature Board of the Australia Council for the Arts, and his poems have been published in journals and anthologies in nine countries.

Nathanael O'Reilly
**Preparations
for Departure**

Poetry

First published in 2017 by
UWA Publishing
Crawley, Western Australia 6009
www.uwap.uwa.edu.au

UWAP is an imprint of UWA Publishing
a division of The University of Western Australia

THE UNIVERSITY OF
WESTERN
AUSTRALIA

National Library of Australia
Cataloguing-in-Publication entry:
O'Reilly, Nathanael, author.
Preparations for departure / Nathanael O'Reilly.
ISBN: 9781742589459 (paperback)
Includes bibliographical references.
Australian poetry—21st century.
Poetry—Collections.

Designed by Becky Chilcott, Chil3
Typeset in Lyon Text by Lasertype
Printed by McPherson's Printing Group

 uwapublishing

For Tricia & Celeste

Contents

Border Crossings

I. Vienna to Brno

As we cross the Danube and leave Vienna
the guy on my left reads every article
in *Le Monde* about the Paris terror.

The girl on my right reads *Harry Potter* in Czech
on her iPad then switches to the film adaptation.
At the Czech border two police officers

board the bus to check passports
while two more stand outside
flirting with the stewardess

as she hands them fresh coffee.
Syrian kids play in the car park
beside the border while their mother

hangs washing on a wire fence.
Across the border we pass casinos
a church on an island in a lake

a billboard featuring a topless woman
covering her breasts with one arm
while using the other to give the finger

to someone outside the frame.
I listen to Nirvana, U2 and Springsteen
as we pass vineyards, tractors ploughing

fields, villages centred around churches
hundreds of windmills generating
guilt-free energy, billboards advertising

Aqualand Moravia. The girl beside me
carries on two text conversations
simultaneously, deftly switching

between Nokia and Samsung.
She falls asleep sixteen k's from Brno
as we pass a subdivision of McMansions

and Hagrid comforts Hermione. A train
rushes past in the opposite direction
as Springsteen growls 'this is your hometown.'

II. Prešov to Bratislava

At Kysak old men drink vodka before departure.
Stacks of Hanjin shipping containers
rust beside crumbling Soviet factories.

Mist hovers above the pine-tree-covered hills.
Patches of snow glint atop mountains.
Cabins reflect in frigid lakes.

Four old ladies talk unceasingly for hours.
Nine young men drink pivo in the dining car
while singing along to folk music

blasting from a cell phone.
A young couple run their hands
through each other's hair and over

the contours of toned taut muscles. Passengers
produce seemingly endless supplies
of bread, meat and cheese from luggage.

The train passes a ruined castle
on a rocky outcrop as I sip whisky
in the dining car. Hundreds

of architecturally identical villages
occupy both sides of the line.
Infrastructure crumbles and rusts

at every station while orange-clad workers
stand in doorways watching with folded arms.
Vegetable gardens and orchards fill the front

and back yards of houses and cottages –
no space wasted on lawns here.
Steep roofs suggest heavy snows.

A man orders a glass of vodka
in the dining car and knocks it back
before the waitress calculates change.

Woodsmoke emanates from chimneys
and drifts away towards forested hills.
Church clocks and bell towers rise above

villages projecting power over the people.
An old woman cuts the queue at the bar.
A young man shrugs and sighs – *This is Slovakia.*

III. Bratislava to Vienna

Changing infrastructure
makes visible the unmarked border
between Slovakia and Austria

as girls beside me converse
in Slovak and read memes
from their iPhones aloud in English.

Grey skies lower above
flat green countryside.
Animals are absent.

A Slovakian girl repeatedly
adjusts her hair while the guy
behind her takes selfies

and laughs at his own image.
Windmills tall as abbeys
cram the horizon.

Green-painted bases
and grey columns support
slowly turning red-striped blades

above ploughed and planted
unfenced fields. A young woman
wears a t-shirt with the word *Zero*

emblazoned in silver across
her breasts, defying reality.
Black leather boots zip

all the way up to her bare knees.
The elderly conductor mutters
and sighs as he checks tickets.

New apartment buildings rise
above fields on the outskirts
of Vienna marking suburbia's edge.

Inside the city, Mercedes,
Audis and BMWs proliferate.
Wealth makes itself visible.

The garden sheds have flowerboxes
and lace curtains in the windows.
A signal box covered in graffiti

says *this city is just like any other*
despite the Danube, Aryan beauty,
waltzes, fur coats, cake and coffee.

Letters painted on a metal fence
proclaim *Arise!* while a *Bauhaus*
sign promises modernity.

Karekare

For Celeste

Rubbing noses
on the beach
at Karekare
bare feet sink
into black sand

looking west
across the Tasman
the misty rain
and salt spray
beads our faces

we listen
to waves breaking
wind singing
black sand drifting
towards home

Lusitanian

My Lusitanian ancestors
could not have imagined
descendants in the Antipodes
with fair skin, blue eyes
and blonde hair, speaking
English, not knowing a word
of their tongue. They lacked
the power to look across
hemispheres and centuries
to foresee that one of their own
would embark alone over oceans
on a journey to a continent
they did not know existed
where she would acquire
a new language, anglicise
her name, abandon
her former identity.

Today's News from The Gulf

Seventy-two Americans confirmed dead
in storm-ravaged states renewing hope
with soap former refugee ropes in hotels

to improve hygiene of millions globally
advertisement for subscribers only
PRIZES WORTH MILLIONS TO BE WON!

SUBSCRIBE TODAY AND BE A WINNER
Arab-American voters unlikely
to back Obama in large numbers

people arrive in droves as RTA marks
third annual Public Transport Day
the Federation was established

to build pillars of security and safety
Riyadh truck explosion kills twenty-two
more than one hundred and ten injured

'Significant' damage as accident
in industrial area engulfs buildings
cars in flames Kuwait warns of stern action

rev it up sold-out fourth Abu Dhabi
F1 Grand Prix at Yas Marina Circuit
authorities in Kuwait warned yesterday

harsher measures crack down
demonstrators defying bans
in the increasingly tense nation

Kuwait last week banned public
gatherings of more than twenty people
PART SALE up to 60% OFF

the outcome seen as pivotal
moment in Kuwait's political showdowns
you are cordially invited to celebrate

the grand launch of your favourite
fashion destination create a fresh
contemporary colonial feel

with this cool calm and collected look
eleven artworks of Fatima and Salama
will be displayed on Marrakesh

commuters walk away with iPads
thousands of people rode the Metro
for the first time and vowed

it wouldn't be their last trip
egged on by a friend he hopped
onto the Metro and simply loved it

snaking queues of people
eager to part with their blood
could be seen since morning

upgrade yourself taxi-sex couple
claim driver lied Dubai police
have arrested two men in a hit

and run incident two Emirati men
were arrested for killing
a Pakistani worker court asked

drop sex public indecency charges
after forensic report fails
to prove sexual activity

lawyer accused a driver
of fabricating story about drunk
couple getting naked and having sex

in backseat of his taxi
confessed to getting drunk
but denied cuddling

Asian man arrested last month
caught using stolen number plates
man caught driving at 271 km/h

police hunting man
three hundred and thirty-seven
law breakers held in Dubai

illegally selling goods on the street
illegally washing cars and begging
violators expected to be deported

Dubai authorities last month rounded
up one hundred and seventy-seven
street vendors one hundred and four

illegal butchers and fish cleaners
forty beggars and sixteen car washers
The Arab League slammed

results of the European Parliament's
report on human rights in the UAE
efforts are being undertaken

to implement the initiative
officer honoured for selfless act
he administered first aid

she regained consciousness
but complained of pain in her legs
witnessed increase in children

seeking psychological counselling
NATION CELEBRATES
December 2 brings back memories

a dear occasion for every citizen recalling
their forefathers' and ancestors'
sacrifices who laid down the foundations

for unity which prompted them to proceed
with the building process
fortify its pillars and grounds

the whole city colours itself
with a spectacular display of light
fireworks impresses Emiratis

expatriates and tourists
the country was able to meet
the necessary educational requirements

for a modern nation-state
gunfire may have caused wedding disaster
television footage and pictures posted

on social media showed a body
lying by burnt-out vehicles
two charred bodies seated in a car

searching for victims in the rubble
covered in dirt and bleeding
multiple cuts over body

fifty-five people injured in tragedy
initial reports said wire may have dropped
onto the door after it was hit by a bullet

in the celebratory fire
that usually accompanies
weddings in rural areas

detained by Saudi authorities
for writing comments
on Twitter about the Quran

held since April without charge
online commentators called
for his arrest and execution

in custody since February 12
for tweets discussing religion
ban on Bahrain rallies temporary

protesters run for cover
as riot police use stun grenades
and tear gas to disperse them

dozens of people especially children
rushed to hospital
after inhaling gases

riot police extensively
used stun grenades and tear gas
on Kylie Minogue, Nickelback and Eminem

All words sourced from the *Gulf News*, November 2nd, 2012

Orange Crush

I first heard REM's Orange Crush
               while shopping
capitalism
chemical warfare
       & cultural imperialism
            came together
in a pop rush ecstasy

Greek Summer

For Tricia

On the road from Patras to Corinth,
I piss in petrol station toilets
paved with marble, eat lamb,
potatoes, tomatoes and feta,
break bread worthy of dreams.

In Delphi, an Orthodox priest
stands in an empty street
smoking a cigarette, waiting
for a funeral to begin.
I chat with hotel workers
in English, their Aussie accents
thicker than mine, broadened
by years driving Sydney taxis.

Lounging on a nightclub sofa
with a view across the valley
of olives beneath Delphi
I sip ouzo, watch American
college kids grind on each other
in rhythm to Usher's beats,
ponder my ageing soul.

On Aegina I rent a Vesper,
gorge myself on olives,
tempt fate in board shorts.

At Sarpas Athena unleashes
her hair, bares brown breasts,
knocks back another Mythos,
submerges in the Saronic.

On Hydra I drink ouzo
with the ghosts of Johnston,
Clift and Cohen, walk
in Winton's footsteps,
follow donkeys through alleys,
fantasise about checking out,
staying on to write novels.

Drinking before dawn
on a Plaka rooftop
with new friends
ten years younger
I miss your presence,
wish you could share
the view, the wine, my bed.

Tahrir Square

February 11th, 2011

The people oust a dictator
　　　in just eighteen days
without resorting to violence
the revolution is televised
　　　live on Al Jazeera
as the crowd dances and sings
in ecstasy and euphoria
civilians embrace soldiers
paint graffiti on tanks
children are lifted into the air
flags waved in jubilation
and the people just can't stop
smiling, struggling to believe
　　　they succeeded at last
and Mubarak has fled
　　　to Sharm el Sheikh
victorious protesters
shout over the music of liberation
into cell phones transmitting
their message live via radio
This is the happiest day of our lives!

In the Marketplace

The beggar-lady sings from under
her umbrella, sitting in the mud
nursing her child in the marketplace.
Tossing some kopeks into her pouch
I hurry on, clashing umbrellas
with shoppers, dodging puddles.

Young and old, men and women,
peasants and townsfolk battle
daily for survival in the marketplace.
I simply observe and pass by,
my needs and survival unthreatened.
To them I am a rich Amerikanski,
an alien from a golden dreamland.

My clothes and accent
proclaim I do not belong
and never will. In three weeks
I'll be gone, back in the West,
eating in restaurants, living
in luxury, while the battlers
in the marketplace remain
to fight for their daily bread.

The Distance Between

After a day exploring Belfast
        with local friends aware
of every boundary and rule
whether visible or invisible
        spoken or unspoken
I finally began to understand
        the distance between
Dublin and Sandy Row

Poet Makes the News

I receive the news from Dublin
while eating breakfast:
Seamus Heaney is dead.

Thoughts turn to Casualty,
Digging and Mid-Term Break,
Shelley on Keats, Auden on Yeats.

Driving to work, the radio on,
I catch Heaney reading the last
line of a poem I am too slow

to recognise. His voice, unexpected,
alive just hours ago, evades
my guard. The tears come,

oozing uninvited for a man
I never met. All morning,
articles, obituaries, videos

of the poet reading his work
arrive in my office, sent
from Europe and North America.

A colleague tells a grand tale
of Heaney teaching her to dance
a reel at a ceilidh in North Carolina.

Every major English-language
news organisation in the world
reports Heaney's passing.

Syria is bumped.
Obama can wait.
Poetry is world news.

I lunch alone, raise a pint of Guinness
in Seamus' honour, read Scaffolding
on my phone in the corner of the pub.

Driving home, Heaney is on the radio
reading The Toome Road
and Paul Muldoon is reminiscing

about meeting Heaney in Armagh.
Muldoon attempts to read Digging,
chokes up, unable to swallow his grief.

Churchill's Black Dog

Bitten by the black dog in London
I made a call to another hemisphere

where a former lover convinced
me to discard the bag of white powder

I was too weak to refuse
in the toilets at The World's End

Soho Proposition

A Jamaican woman wearing
a fake Burberry
leans against a Soho doorframe
beckons fingers curling

What kin' of girl you want?
Asian, Black, Russian, Chinese?
We got dem all, mon.

I push my hands deeper
into jacket pockets
hunch shoulders
against drizzle
catch her eye
move farther
into the darkness

Bath Scenes

Houseboats wait to pass
through the Weston locks
as ducks glide upon the Avon

morning drinkers on their benches
under the willow trees sip cans
of Foster's watching cyclists pass

a seagull swoops into the beer
garden and swipes a Yorkshire
pudding from a startled diner

flies away triumphantly
as Sunday afternoon drinkers
laugh, nudge and point

the temperature reaches
twenty degrees Celsius – *A scorcher!*
declares the radio DJ –

and parks fill with women in bikinis
shirtless middle-aged men
teenagers drinking cheap cider

elderly couples lying on blankets
kids kicking footballs to fathers
a family eating homemade pasties

notes from a busker's saxophone
drift through Abbey Square
towards Roman Baths tourists

a scowling homeless man crouches
beside an ATM daring the cashless
to withdraw without making a deposit

old blokes in the Crystal Palace argue
about the best way to get to Gloucester
as wives sip Pimms, roll eyes

a middle-aged bald man in a bespoke suit
caresses his partner's stocking-sheathed
thigh as she checks the train schedule

declares there's time for one more
round as he bounds to the bar
orders her a double of Jameson's

in the bookstore basement bibliophiles
crawl searching the lowest shelves
for poetry and journals of exploration

at the bus stop young women gaze
upon shirtless men demolishing
a building across the street

the Bed & Breakfast owner steps
outside, lights a cigarette
leans his shoulder against

the stone portico wall
takes a deep drag then spits
brown saliva over his wife's flowers

a workman carries a naked
mannequin from a shop and throws
her headfirst into a Transit van

two old ladies bent double
on the bus stop bench
laugh their guts up

the day after Halloween
a cracked vampire mask
lies abandoned in an alley

a nine-year-old girl turns consecutive
cartwheels on Solsbury Hill
before the summer solstice sunset

a taxi driver parked
outside The Harington Club
blasts It's Not Unusual

Walking from Fulmer to Gerrards Cross

Uphill all the way
blue hands clench
deep inside coat pockets

shoulders hunch forward
as Antipodean melodies
crackle through headphones

drops of misty rain
bead on a woollen scarf
droop from earlobes

low grey foreign skies
smother lush green fields
bisected by the motorway

cracked leather boots squeak
faded corduroy trousers swish
ageing knees & ankles crack

farm buildings & cottages
double-storeyed detached houses
behind stone walls & hedges

yield to former council estates
modest semidetached dwellings
petrol stations & pubs

on the High Street
cafes restaurants boutiques
huddle together

face each other
on the way
to the railway station

Solitude

Travelling backwards from Bath to Dorchester
through Freshford, Bradford on Avon, Trowbridge,
Westbury, Castle Cary, Yeovil and Maiden Newton,
over hills, through vales, across meads,
reading *Time's Laughingstocks*
I delve into the heart of Hardy's Wessex.

Morning sun glistens on green grass,
cows graze in the shadow of hedgerows,
freshly shorn sheep lounge on hillsides.
I pass harvested fields, baled hay, falling leaves,
ripening apples, stone cottages with slate roofs.

I walk from Dorchester to Stinsford
beside the gurgling water, visit
Hardy's grave at St Michael's,
explore the church interior,
stand alone at the pulpit
declaiming from the Book of Job.

Through fields and woods I hike
to Higher Bockhampton, stopping
in Thorncombe Wood for sandwiches
beside Hardy's birthplace, then onwards
across the Roman Road to Lower Bockhampton.
Crossing the Froom I pass freshly mowed
fields following Hardy's footsteps to Max Gate.

After a pick-me-up pint at the Trumpet Major
I stroll back into the centre of Dorchester,
explore the ruins of a Roman villa at dusk,
marvel at intact third-century mosaics
before retiring for dinner at The Royal Oak.

LAX Jetlag

Holed up at an airport hotel
for twenty-four hours trying
to conquer jetlag

with the curtains drawn
and a Do Not Disturb sign
on the door, I lie wide

awake at two a.m. local time
willing my body to adapt
to the new time zone

I contemplate going down
to the twenty-four-hour gym
running on the treadmill

until reaching exhaustion
I reach for the duty-free
on the night-stand

grab the remote
turn on the television
mutter *fuck it*

Bayswater

Returning to my girlfriend's
after searching
all day for work
I find my backpack
abandoned
on the front steps

The note pinned
to the side-pocket
unnecessary – the message
clear – *Went out for drinks*

Last night I lay
on a couch in the corner
of her flatmate's room
facing the wall attempting
sleep while he loudly
enjoyed the favours
of his Swedish girlfriend

Under the weight of my luggage
I shuffle down Queensway
towards Kensington Gardens
in search of a quiet place to lie

BBQ

Standing in a dirt lot on Cesar Chavez
waiting to order brisket at La Barbecue

we sip on local brews purchased
at the convenience store on the corner

make friends with our neighbours
from Perth, London and New Jersey

sweat drips inside our t-shirts, slides
down our arms, saturates socks

as we crack open our third beer
after an hour in line, finally

we receive our pound of brisket
potato salad and pickles, eat

at a picnic table with our newfound
community and savour meat slow-cooked

for sixteen hours, trading travel tales
we commune and imbibe, share

recommendations and discover connections
remember food always opens the door

Canadian Drinking Sessions

For J. B.

Discussing poetry in hotel bars
in Montreal, Toronto & Calgary
we drank whiskey & argued
ceremonially about who would pay

Drinking pints in Toronto
summer sun – outside English
pubs on streets with Scottish
names – our hemispheres merged

Commandment

On a West Texas highway
between Plainview and Lubbock

white text on a black billboard
proclaims *CONTROL YOUR MIND,*

OR THE DEVIL WILL!
urging passing drivers

and passengers to exert
self-control, search souls

flee from temptation
banish impure thoughts

refrain from coveting
thy neighbour's truck

think righteous thoughts
in the service of fear

Packing for Camping in New Mexico

carry the tent, mattresses and blankets
down from the attic above the garage

set up the tent in the backyard
check for missing pieces and holes

gather sleeping bags, backpacks
folding chairs, coolers, hiking boots

pack backpacks with hiking clothes
swimsuits, long-sleeved tops and pants

for cool mountain mornings
evenings relaxing by the fire

pack sunscreen, toiletries and insect
repellent – don't forget the bear

pepper spray, matches or torches
fill the coolers with water bottles

beer, tonic water, fruit, juice
vegies – fill woven shopping bags

with cooking utensils, canned
beans and tomatoes, tortillas
pasta, rice, power bars, trail mix

blue agave, salsa, corn chips
gin, whisky and coffee

bring novels, poetry collections
the chess set and a deck of cards

load everything into the SUV
don't forget the axe

hammer, handsaw and pocket knife
bring Lyle Lovett, Dylan, Counting Crows

for the nine-hour drive
to the Santa Fe National Forest

finally, check the tyre pressure
oil and water levels, fill the fuel

tank, drive northwest to freedom

Resorting

A band plays calypso
and reggae beside the pool

while sunbathing adults
sip sapphire margaritas

kids play with beach balls
teens parade round the water's edge

lifeguards nod in time
step back and forth poolside

grandparents take refuge
in the shade of turquoise

yellow and orange umbrellas
boys sword-fight with noodles

parents survey toddlers in the shallows
mothers rub sunscreen

into impatient young skin
palm fronds undulate lazily

like tipsy dancers, shadows
slide slowly across the pool

tween girls strut like teen girls
white clouds stagnate in blue skies

lethargic as humans amidst humidity
swaggering tween boys flex muscles

present only in dreams, hairy-backed
men feign Chewbacca cool

women check out other women
scanning for imperfections

middle-aged men chase youth
down the waterslide

Ruskin's View

I sip a pint of Hartley's Cambrian Way
in the Red Dragon in Kirkby Lonsdale

before walking through St Mary's graveyard
to Ruskin's View, painted by Turner and judged

by the critic to be *one of the loveliest views
in England, therefore in the world.*

Gazing upon the River Lune, stone walls,
meadows, fields, woods, Wharton Farm,

Casterton and High Casterton,
I find it impossible to be unimpressed

and the Anglocentric arrogance
of Ruskin's proclamation seems forgivable

as time passes like the shadows of clouds
across the peaks of Gragareth and Ingleborough.

Transnational Panorama

Running on the Cotswolds
Way I splash through ankle-deep

mud uphill along the public
footpath between stone walls,

hedges, barbed wire and electric
fences, shimmy through kissing

gates between fields and forests,
slip on piles of autumn leaves,

fight inclines, wind and rocks
on my way to the highest point,

look down over Bath, Weston,
Kelston, Swineford and Saltford

across luminous green fields,
brown hedgerows and copses,

the Avon and the Severn
all the way to Wales.

Transcarpathia

I.
We spent a summer late
last century in the former
USSR at the confluence

of the Tiza and Rika rivers
living in a Transcarpathian
valley with the mafia

the unemployed and the future
our students guided us
around town, to the castle

ruins, Gorodskoy park
the outdoor markets
and the plains of blood

accompanied us to neighbouring
villages, towns and cities
Rokosovo, Velyatyn, and Uzhgorod

we shot vodka with our principal
students' parents, government officials
and gangsters, afraid to offend

our students competed for turns
to sweep the classroom floor
clean the blackboard, read aloud

take us swimming after classes
have coffee with us in cafes
serve us dinner in their homes

II.
we arrived by train at the Hungarian–
Ukrainian border in the darkness
met our driver on the platform

loaded our luggage into his ancient
van and took our seats beside
curtain-covered windows

for the drive from Chop to Khust
through the unknown over potholes
to a pumping techno soundtrack

disoriented and alien, we arrived
in town near midnight, met hosts
who insisted on measuring us

before unloading, eating and drinking
declared our unusual Western height
qualified us for double rations

III.
reading a novel in Gorodskoy
park I was approached
by local gangsters who took

up positions in front and behind
pistols tucked conspicuously
into tracksuit pants waistbands

demanded to know my business
and nationality before deciding
I was harmless, the leader

making homophobic jokes
in English about his comrade
my faggot buddy doesn't understand

before inviting me to their bar
where we played pool in the basement
drank pivo with the local boss

IV.
local gang members climbed
our dark stairwell, pounded
on our steel door, demanded

in urgent fragmented English
that we come outside
hand over our passports

inside we stood silently still
against cracked walls
waiting for danger to fade

V.
every weekday morning we walked
to school, past government offices
empty storefronts, crumbling

Soviet-built apartment blocks
past Romanian gypsies sitting
in the dirt begging for kopeks

across the Mlynovytsya river
past groups of kids yelling
Hey, fuck you buddy!

Hey, suck my dick, buddy!
mimicking Hollywood
bad-guy rhetoric

collecting our students
in ones and twos as we walked
we arrived at school in a gang

VI.
on scorching hot afternoons
our students took us to the Tisa
served us packed picnic lunches

cooked pig fat on sticks over fires
lit in the sand, ganged up
and threw us in the river

jumped with us off the abandoned
railway bridge into dangerous water
vying for our admiration

the teenage girls wore tiny bikinis
the teenage boys wore speedos
called us gypsies for wearing shorts

exhausted after swimming
we sat cross-legged on the sand
in a circle while Sasha played

Nirvana covers on his battered
acoustic guitar and the girls
sang mournful folk songs

VII.
on the road to Lviv
miles from the nearest village
we passed a Babushka

head covered in traditional
fashion, sitting on the ground
beside an upturned bucket

a lone cabbage perched atop
patiently waiting in the heat
to make the day's final sale

VIII.
we walked unpaved dusty streets
occasionally passed by a vehicle
a local riding in an engineless

Lada or Volga towed by a donkey
or a tracksuit-clad mafia man
driving a late-model BMW

IX.
the majority of the town's men
unemployed filled their days
drinking vodka outside cafes

until they passed out with heads
and arms on tables or fell sideways
from plastic chairs onto concrete

the town's women went to market
haggled over the price of bread
cabbage and potatoes, desperate

to save precious gryvnya
and kopeks, unable to afford
luxuries like meat or fruit

X.
late at night we wandered home
from cafes and friends' apartments
down narrow brick-paved streets

past abandoned Soviet army trucks
across the Khustet's River
through the square where Father

Lenin's statue stood, past the war
memorial, onion-domed
icon-filled Orthodox churches

concrete-block houses under construction
grassless front yards full of precious
cabbages, potatoes and onions

XI.
students' parents took us in
to their homes, told us tales
of their lives under Soviet rule

showed us family albums of holidays
to Odessa and Chornomorsk
kids frolicking on Black Sea sand

taught us their post-independence
mantra: *under communism, we had jobs,*
we had money, but there was nothing

to buy – now we have no jobs
we have no money
and there's still nothing to buy!

XII.
on the train to Solotvyno we followed
the Ukrainian–Romanian border
southeast, barbed wire always

within view outside the right-hand
train windows, soldiers gripping machine
guns in guard towers watching over

the border, ready to kill if necessary
identically dressed peasants working
the fields either side of the border

XIII.
at Solotvyno we walked from the station
through unpaved village streets
browsed stores selling icons

purchased wooden jewellery, crosses
necklaces, bracelets and blouses
before arriving at the salt lakes

we floated on our backs in dark water
slathered each other in black mud
erased each other's identities

XIV.
on Voloshyna, Lvivska and Ivana Franka
students, friends and acquaintances
crossed the street to shake hands

men and boys kissed us
on the cheeks declaring affection
signalling their importance

as buddies of the Australianski
and Canadianski, local television
reporters stopped us on Karpatskoyi

to conduct interviews
Who are you? Why are you here?
Do you like our country?

XV.
on my twenty-fourth birthday
my students decorated
our classroom with banners

before my arrival, sang
Happy Birthday in English,
presented me with a gift

they purchased collectively:
a plastic mantel-piece-sized
Swiss clock replica

upon my departure
the clock was confiscated
at the Hungarian border

along with landscape paintings
gifts from students and parents
all declared National Treasures

by Ukrainian customs officials
too precious for export, worth
a few gryvnya on the black market

XVI.
on the road to Lviv we passed
an abandoned nuclear power plant
ten times the size of any American mall

a VISA billboard between the road
and a wheat field proclaimed
IT'S EVERYWHERE YOU WANT TO BE

defying reality and our experience
an advance party advocate for capitalism
convenience and Westernisation

Ode to a Coffee Pot

Ah, Bodum! For two decades
you have travelled across the seas
my constant portable companion
dwelt with me on three continents
and never ceased to provide
       comfort when called upon

together we crossed the Széchenyi
endured American autumns in exile
survived a London winter in poverty
enjoyed marvellous homecomings

I gently spoon freshly ground
Colombian coffee into you
and fill you with boiling water
let you brew on your own
allow you to take your time
like a teenage girl smoking
       on the front step
of a run-down milk bar
before pressing your plunger
slowly towards your base

together we make lovely liquid
smooth as the fleece of a vicuña
let us continue collaborating
      far into the future
I will continue to protect you
      whether journeying
      or staying home

Newlywed

For Tricia

During our first year together, we moved
into the first of three apartments in Texas,
between the highway and the railway,
where we lay listening to oil rumble past
in the night bound for Gulf Coast refineries.

Your bike was stolen from its resting place
near the dumpster by a Taco Bell worker
who strapped a radio to the frame and rode
it blatantly around town. We walked
across the highway to the video store
where they knew our names and stopped
at the Fina for chips and six-packs of beer.

We drove to the County Court House to obtain
our marriage licence. The civil ceremony
was conducted business-like with co-workers
as witnesses in the county clerk's office,
an empty coke can on the officiant's desk,
a portrait of a SWAT team on the wall.

We played cards on Thursday nights
in a single-wide trailer with friends,
beer, cigars and Stevie Ray. We drove
to Shreveport to play the loosest slots
in Louisiana, gorge on the buffet.

We spent weekends in Austin
and San Antonio lounging by the pool,
washed down fajitas with margaritas.
On Friday nights we watched your students
cheer and play football. On Sundays,
we played Pac-Man at the Laundromat.
On sultry summer evenings
we swam naked in the lake.

Locating Satellites

Locating satellites
the watch declares
as muscles are stretched
earbuds adjusted
music begins
a series of zeros
signals readiness

as always the right foot
steps off the driveway first
the left foot follows
entering the rhythm
joined by loosely clenched fists
arms alternately swinging
repeat repeat repeat

lit by the rising sun
garbage waits by the curb
pick-ups, SUVs and sedans
back out of driveways
conveying coffee-sipping
smartphone-gripping
commuters to work

clumps of kids wait
on corners for the bus
backpacks strewn at feet
boys eyeing girls eyeing boys

damp hair freshly styled
hands deep in pockets
breath rising like desire

beyond the subdivision's limits
out on the open road
shoes pass broken beer bottles
discarded fast-food wrappers
pink and white striped underwear
undisturbed for months
becoming landscape

sun glints off oil tanks
passing shale trucks flatten grass
the medical centre's digital sign
alternates between time
temperature, opening hours
phone numbers, *ACCEPTING NEW
PATIENTS, WALK-INS WELCOME*

delivery trucks reverse
towards supermarket loading bays
the parking lot at the strip mall
begins to fill with workers' vehicles
the line at the donut shop
drive-through window stretches
back to the road, blocks the sidewalk

the left foot follows the right
lungs inhale exhale
digits on the watch face
change ceaselessly
tracking time distance pace
the miles stretch ahead
fall away behind
repeat repeat repeat

Hovering

A hummingbird hovers
outside my window
inches from the glass

eyes level we observe
each other for a long minute
before the hummingbird

returns to the flowers
on the trumpet vine
hovering and imbibing

beside the fattening bees
as rain drips from the eaves
slides down leaves

A Glance, a Sigh

Pausing during the exam
the student places her thumb
inside the collar of her shirt
pulls cotton away from skin
glances down at her breasts

satisfied, she sighs softly
picks up her pen, and resumes

Overhead on Campus

A found poem

Lavender shorts are *tight*
my straps are a little loose
I hate, hate, *hate*
wearing skirts

I'm like, the only one
who did all the reading
if you want, you can come
to the library with me

I'm a little bit concerned
about the whole West Nile thing –
five people have died already
well, that *is* a blessing

I can't wait to slam him
on the evaluations –
he's always pushing
his liberal agenda

have you seen this PETA video?
it's the saddest thing ever
I literally cried
OhMyGod

is she even thankful that I did that?
she was only on her first bottle
it was a long night –
I've blocked most of it out

are you going to the party
tonight? lucky son of a bitch
Wow. You blame me for that?!
you couldn't pay me to be an RA

you're not moving my shit!
I'm about to fucking lose it
I *do not* want to deviate from the plan
I only had two hours sleep last night!

I'm tired as fuck...Did you
just say what I think you said?!
I love you
text me during class!

Mid-Term Exam

knuckles crack   nostrils sniff
lungs cough   chairs creak
pencils scratch   arms stretch

    fingers brush back hair
    chests rise and fall
    fingertips stroke chins

paper rustles   erasers erase
pages turn   eyes glance

    the EXIT sign winks
    legs cross & uncross
    elbows rest on desks

tongues lick lips
mouths stretch wide yawning
pens   race   right   across   the   page

    central heating hums
    distant voices echo in the hall
    the second hand advances relentlessly

Cazaly

Listening to the seven-inch
    of Up There Cazaly
in the bedroom of the kid
    from across the road
after school on a winter afternoon
    in nineteen seventy-nine
we wore our jerseys with pride
    handballed the Sherrin
back and forth as we belted
    out the chorus
unabashed innocent
    children of the decade

The Way We Saw Ourselves

For Chris Barnes

Do you remember the day,
our last day together before
we left home and grew up?
When we sat on the roof
of your parents' house drinking
cheap port and listening
to Pink Floyd albums?

Years ago now, those days
when the world seemed ours
for the taking, when we dreamt
wildly, full of hope
and our own importance.

Years later, I marvel
at the way we saw ourselves.

January Light

I discovered my purpose
        during summer weeks

surviving on white wine
        bread and cheese

imbibing Lawrence
        Orwell and Hardy

reclining on a Chesterfield
        in a secluded room

behind blinds closed
        against January light

Porridge

We lived for days on Nescafe Blend 43
and porridge sprinkled with brown sugar
denying ourselves like old-age pensioners
making ten bucks span the distance
between Saturday night's pub crawl
and the fortnightly Austudy payment.

We stayed home in our damp mouldy flat
huddled in stained sleeping bags reading
photocopied required texts, unable to afford
to fire up the gas heater. Twice a month
we walked to the Westpac ATM
emptied our accounts, paid the rent
put some money aside for the phone
and utilities bills, bought our groceries
then blew most of the rest at the bottle shop.

Arms full of bottles in brown paper bags
we shuffled through autumn leaves
like deros heading for a bench, anticipating
the burn of the tawny port and the relief
of the warmth spreading from within.

Lost

After driving to Daylesford
       through soft drizzle
I stand beside the lake
       beads of water gathering on my hair
       sliding slowly
           down my face
as I watch the ducks dive
       contemplate all I've lost

Daylesford

For Toby

Dressed in a three-piece suit
purchased from an op shop
you recited Auden's Lullaby
as we drove from Ballarat
to your twin cottages
beside the lake at Daylesford.

While your Labrador panted
by the fire we sipped tea
and browsed a book
on Australian art, pausing
to examine pages devoted
to your late father's work.

Wearing Hard Yakka overalls
your partner joined us, pregnant
with the child you conceived
on the slopes of Mount Franklin.

After we finished our drinks,
you took me next door
to your other cottage
where I was stunned to find
every room full of books.

You found *The English Patient,*
told me it won the Booker
and insisted I read it, that contrary
to our lecturer's belief, literature
published after 1950 is worth reading.

Sixteen years later, I returned
and found a bookstore beside the lake
but couldn't find a trace of you.

Castlemaine

Driving through deserted
Castlemaine streets after
midnight on the way

home to Bendigo singing
REM's Driver 8
I wind my window

down inches
to receive June air
after a sleepless weekend

spent with dear friends
drinking dancing laughing
I revel in possibilities

in the early morning hours
driving alone through darkness
towards an invisible horizon

Cold Beer & Company

In the small country towns
left over from the goldrush
the verandahs of the shops
       cover the footpaths
providing shady sanctuaries
on scorching summer afternoons
for those who dare to venture
from cool interiors in pursuit
of cold beer & company
     at the corner hotel

Castlereagh

Limping along Castlereagh Street
after drinking in the city all day
turning vowels over in my mind
I considered the name that captivated

poets from Paterson to Slessor
to James, the name the street
shared with a suburb, a river
a town in County Down

and a viscount who incurred
the wrath of Byron and Shelley.

Weeks later, with the vowels
still echoing around my brain
I arrived in Coonabarabran
a town built on the river

named Castlereagh.
I ate a picnic lunch beside
the water while my daughter
climbed and ran in the park

where I first heard the word
more than three decades ago.

Projecting Nonchalance

During long afternoons
in Australian cities
I kept teenage girls
and young women company
as they shopped for clothes
at Myer in Melbourne
Just Jeans in Brisbane
Cotton On in Ballarat

Valued for patience
(and occasionally good taste)
I loitered outside women's
dressing rooms, fetched
different sizes and colours
answered in muted tones
when eagerly questioned
How does this look?

Shop assistants mistook
me for a boyfriend
when I was summoned
to a stall and invited
to carefully consider
the degree of snugness
of a pair of jeans
projecting nonchalance

Burning Patiently

With apologies to Pablo Neruda

We caught a cab to the club
and found a table outside
where we got started with g & t's

She wore knee-high leather boots
black hip-hugging low-rise pants
a sleeveless lacy low-cut blouse

with a flesh-coloured lining
creating the illusion of nudity
beneath diaphanous material

when the DJ played Discotheque
we pushed our way to the dance floor
gyrated sweatily to the rhythms

lost our inhibitions for minutes
before a song we didn't know
brought us back to the present

in the early hours we rode
a taxi home, her head in my lap
my hand unfulfilled in her hair

desire burning patiently towards dawn

This is Serious

Dressed in socks
& a backless gown
I lie on my back

as the nurse covers
me in warm blankets
attaches a heart rate

monitor to my left index
finger & inserts a needle
into a vein in my right wrist

connecting me to an IV drip
as another nurse enters
the room with clipboard & pen

What is your full name?
What is your date of birth?
What procedure are you having today?

having passed the test
Billy & Judy wheel me down
the corridor as a list of drugs

I can't pronounce enters my veins
I pass beneath fluorescent
lights & ageing ceiling tiles

faces crowned by sanitary caps
above blue scrubs look down
declaring *this is serious*

in the operating room the surgeon
pats my shoulder like we're buddies
You'll be just fine, my man

as Billy rolls me on
to the operating table
& I lose consciousness

Inferno

A parked car burns
in Woolloomooloo
at one a.m. on Monday
as I walk home after a night
at The Victoria Room
drinking gin and tonics
with an easy friend
on an antique couch
beneath a trapeze artist
clad in suspenders
and red leather trousers
an arm's reach
from an almost-nude
smiling pole dancer
watching the hipsters swing
to songs sung by a sultry girl
flaunting a flapper dress
backed by bearded men
grooving in vintage suits
playing upright bass
drums and acoustic guitar
in a blues/jazz/folk fusion
revelling in their embrace
of the pseudo-American

cops nonchalantly
watch the burning car
chat casually as smoke spirals
drifts towards the harbour
while I pass the inferno
striding north to water

Wet Wool

Drying off in front of the fire
after being caught in the rain

the smell of wet wool
transports me back

to the mid-eighties
and a classroom in winter

the smell of wet wool
emanating from the jumper

and tartan skirt of the girl
sitting beside me in class

the girl who kissed me
on the cheek in front of everyone

as we lined up before music
the girl who draped her arm

casually around my shoulders
the girl I followed on my bike

and yearned to take for a walk
sit with in the darkening cinema

the girl who sat behind me
at a concert in St Kilda

in nineteen ninety-two
wearing a tartan skirt

and failed to recognise me
when I finally caught her eye

Sydney from a 737

With apologies to Paul Kelly

As the plane banks
curls northeast
towards the harbour

above the Parramatta
I look down on cricket
rugby & soccer fields

backyard swimming pools
red-tiled roofs
Rosehill Racecourse

yachts & pleasure cruisers
moored in coves & bays
traffic sliding across bridges

along freeways & main roads
suburbia stretching
towards the Blue Mountains

descending into the airport
signs on shopfronts proclaim
PANEL BEATING & KUNG FU

Scent Disappointment

Standing in a queue
at the circulation desk
waiting to borrow
The Interpretation of Dreams

I smell your unmistakable
scent. Blood surges
throughout my body
even though I know

you are a thirty-hour drive
away and could not possibly
be standing behind me
in the library

as the scent triggers
memories of skin, teeth
and lips I slowly turn
to look at a girl

who can be nothing
but a disappointment

Contact

An Indigenous man
wearing ceremonial face paint
& a white man dressed
as Captain Cook
chat about the weather
& business, exchanging
laughs & smiles
at Circular Quay
mates for moments
before Bennelong returns
to his didgeridoo
pimping his CD
posing for photos
while Captain Cook
goes back
to spruiking tickets
for cruises on the harbour

Transportation

Hearing Us3's Cantaloop
playing over the sound system
in a Texas gym's locker room

I am transported back
twenty-two years to a restaurant
on Russell Street in Melbourne

eating Lebanese-Italian cuisine
with an almost-girlfriend
at a table near the kitchen

trams rattling by through the rain
droplets sliding down the window
couscous and rosemary rousing senses

conversing about dreams
her masseuse's hands
inches from mine

caressing her wineglass
our knees almost touching
beneath the linen tablecloth

her tongue gently licking
crumbs from her gorgeous lips
her eyes indecipherable

Melbourne Scenes

I.
Lingering in a bar in Williamstown
watching Steve Waugh's final innings
with strangers, a newly formed
community hopes for one
last century before retirement.

II.
Stopping off in Young & Jackson's
for a few pots and a glimpse of Chloe
before catching the train home
lonely bachelors momentarily
possess satisfaction and beauty.

III.
Lying on the beach at St Kilda
nubile youth rub sunscreen
into each other's hot skin
to a soundtrack of joyful screams
from the Luna Park roller-coaster.

IV.
Watching the interstate train
arrive at Platform Number One
as crowds move to and from
Spencer Street, alighting from trams
surging across Bourke Street
hurrying home in June twilight
with newspapers under arms

and collars turned up against
the approaching chill of night
the conductor smokes a cigarette.

V.
Crossing Princes Bridge
hand in hand, new lovers
high on adrenaline, youth
and infatuation perceive
the city and the night
as the most beautiful time
and place imaginable –
the clatter of trams, the click
of high heels and the blast
of taxi horns become sublime.

After the Funeral

For Chris

Dinner at the Hog's Breath Cafe
in Geelong on a weekday evening
less than six hours after burying
our grandmother seems absurd

yet the cold deserted street
the stars and moon obscured
by clouds and the soft drizzle
falling on us feels perfect

My Inheritance

In my dreams I inhabit the paddocks
of my youth, broad expanses
of brown grass divided
by barbed-wire fences, scattered
with droppings and dung.

Riding on the monster tractor
with my grandfather
I revelled in the wind
drawing tears from my eyes.

I sucked in the smell
of the sheep and cows
musty hay, molasses
diesel and wheat.

I ran with the dogs
chasing sheep
from where they grazed
but they were only briefly disturbed
soon settling down to fresh grass.

Between sunrise and bedtime
I lived an eternity, played
and worked, learnt and feasted.
My grandfather's land became my land.

In my mind the hot north wind
still flattens the brown grass
and carries the smell of sheep
and earth across the Pacific.

Six Poets

Six poets drinking wine
in Jimmy Watson's
        discuss poetics
submission strategies
other poets' latest books
the likelihood of acceptance
        by Publisher X
the ideal amount of time
between composition
        & submission
whether one can publish
too much too soon or too often
('the Kinsella effect')
        stimuli & imagination
revision & editing techniques
        the need for varied experience
John Leonard's unerring eye
        who will be read
fifty years from now

Surface

I'm too old now
to honestly say I'm young

and our bodies are moving
farther and farther away

from who we think we are

we look in the mirror
and no longer recognise ourselves

worry about sagging damaged skin
even though we want to believe
our minds are all that matter

Beach Bonding

For Celeste

Driving along the Dingle Peninsula
we turn off the road from Annascaul
to Derrymore, follow a narrow lane
towards the ocean, find ourselves
in a car park in view of the beach
follow a fast-flowing stream down
towards its mouth, where fresh
water meets salt, land meets sea

stepping onto the beach, you run ahead
towards the ocean over sand drifts
seaweed, dune grass and driftwood
arms raised and spread wide with joy
long brown hair blowing eastward

at the water's edge, you wait for me
to arrive, then together we stand
scanning the horizon, first west
where mountains blend into the sea
beneath blue skies and white clouds
sun shining on the eastern slopes
then straight out to sea, spotting
a freighter nearing the end
of its transatlantic crossing
then east where the bay curves
to the left of our vision and low
hills seem to blend into the horizon

we have the beach all to ourselves
on this late December morning
and the only sounds are breaking waves
the Atlantic wind rustling clothing
and our boots squeaking in the sand

you select shells for your international
collection while I take photographs
as we walk along the water's edge
through wet sand, dodging inch-high waves

I tell stories about our ancestors
leaving this island on ships long ago
abandoning loved ones and homes
driven by desperation and dreams

until the wind turns our lips blue
and we head back towards the car
but not before you choose the perfect
piece of driftwood, bend towards
the sand, write *C + N was here*

Distance

We are apart for the fifth time this year –
you're twenty flying hours away
and neither of us is home.

I drink alone and study your photograph
yearn for your return and hope
your desire is only for me.

The distance causes doubt –
how could a woman so intelligent
so beautiful, so sexy, so sophisticated

possibly settle for me, an ageing
inhibited man who doesn't dance
and takes everything too seriously?

I picture you sleeping in clean
white hotel sheets, wonder
which underwear you're wearing

remember the details of your body
the scar beneath your clavicle
the curve of your lower back.

I recall the rhythm of your breath
in the moments before you fall
asleep with our fingers entwined.

I sit in the darkness imagining
the details of your day – where you went
what you wore, what you ate, who you met –

all the things I will never really know.
I fill the days of your absence
with poetry, housework, running

fatherhood, museums, exploration –
trying to enjoy the present
haunted by absence and distance.

Less Light

For Cody Todd (1978-2016)

A bright star has gone out
there is less light in the world

one less poet, teacher, husband,
son, brother to illuminate our lives

no more will your spoken words
cut through the bullshit

no more will your spontaneous
insight see inside the darkness

but your written words will
continue expanding the boundaries

of our universe, immortal
on our bookshelves

reverberating in our minds
Forever singing & dancing

your last Facebook post read
Goodbye champ, we will miss you

I cannot improve on your words

'Forever singing & dancing' is from Cody Todd's poem 'Epistle From the Guild of
Lost Angels'

Preparations for Departure

Born half a mile
            from the Southern Ocean
with salt in the air

and seagulls on the wind
            I am drawn to the edges
of the world   always

making preparations
            for departure.   Unable
to attain belonging

I exist in-between
                        permanently
unsettled and exiled

Acknowledgements

Special thanks to Tricia Jenkins and Lachlan Brown for their insightful feedback on earlier versions of this book. Thanks also to Paul & Moira O'Reilly, Sean Scarisbrick, Alex Lemon, Stuart Barnes, Daniel Young, Nigel Featherstone, Michele Seminara, David Adès, Katherine Gallagher, Jonathan Bennett, Paul Kane, Libby Charlton, Lyn McCredden, Michelle Cahill, Robbie Coburn, Nicholas Birns, Dan Disney, Matt Hetherington, Kit Kelen, Aidan Coleman, Anne Gleeson, David Gilbey, Kent McCarter, Peter Kirkpatrick, David McCooey, Justin Lowe, Mark Roberts, Peter Kilroy, Simon Sleight, Ian Henderson, Pradeep Trikha, Anuraag Sharma, Kris Hemensley, Martina Horakova, Jaroslav Kusnir, Eva Forintos, Cecilia Gall and Andrea Szabo for friendship, support, encouragement, opportunities and inspiration.

Many of the poems in this collection have been published previously, sometimes in a slightly different form. I am extremely grateful to the editors of the following publications: *Postcolonial Text, Verity La, Bluepepper, Transnational Literature, Poetry and Place Anthology 2015, Tincture, Blackmail Press, Social Alternatives, The Disappearing, Windmills, Prosopisia, The Second Genesis: An Anthology of Contemporary World Poetry, Illya's Honey, FourW twenty-five, FourW twenty-seven, Writ Poetry Review* and *Snorkel*.